BLURRED LINES	2	Robin Thicke
DAYLIGHT	7	Maroon 5
GET LUCKY	13	Daft Punk featuring Pharrell Williams
THE HANGMAN'S BODY COUNT	22	Volbeat
JUST GIVE ME A REASON	28	Pink featuring Nate Ruess
LOCKED OUT OF HEAVEN	34	Bruno Mars
NEXT TO ME	42	Emeli Sande
PANIC STATION	49	Muse
RADIOACTIVE	54	Imagine Dragons
STILL INTO YOU	58	Paramore
SUIT & TIE	62	Justin Timberlake
WE ARE YOUNG	72	fun. featuring Janelle Monae
	77	Bass Notation Legend

ISBN 978-1-4803-5354-1

7777 W. BLUEMOUND RD. P.O. BOX 13819 MILWAUKEE, WI 53213

For all works contained herein:
Unauthorized copying, arranging, adapting, recording, Internet posting, public performance,
or other distribution of the printed music in this publication is an infringement of copyright.
Infringers are liable under the law.

Visit Hal Leonard Online at
www.halleonard.com

Blurred Lines

from Robin Thicke - *Blurred Lines*

Words and Music by Pharrell Williams and Robin Thicke

Intro
Moderately ♩ = 116

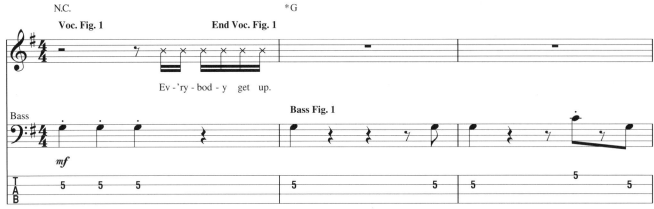

*Chord symbols reflect implied harmony.

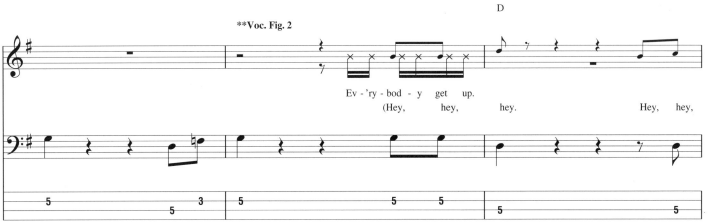

**Refers to upstemmed notes only.

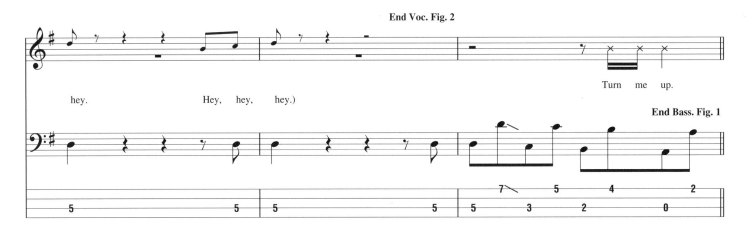

Verse
Bass: w/ Bass Fig. 1 (2 times)

1. If you can't hear what I'm try'n to say, if you can't read
2. What do they make dreams for when you got them jeans on? What do we need steam for?

© 2013 EMI APRIL MUSIC INC., MORE WATER FROM NAZARETH and I LIKE 'EM THICKE MUSIC
All Rights for MORE WATER FROM NAZARETH Controlled and Administered by EMI APRIL MUSIC INC.
All Rights Reserved   International Copyright Secured   Used by Permission

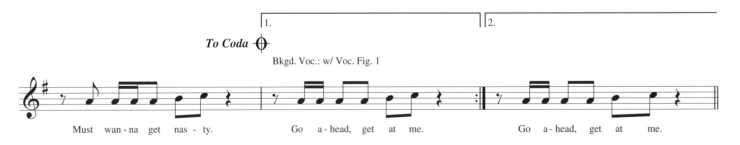

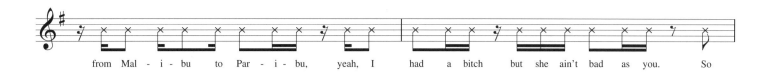
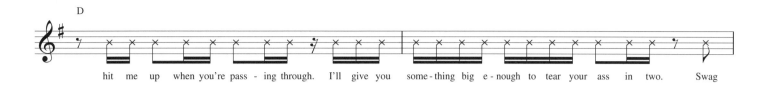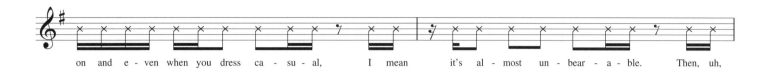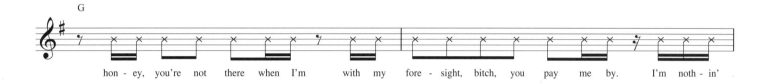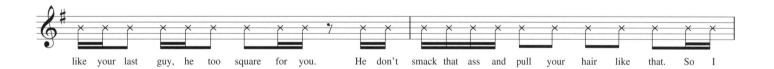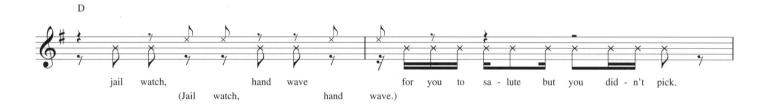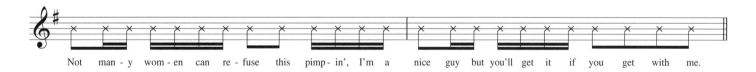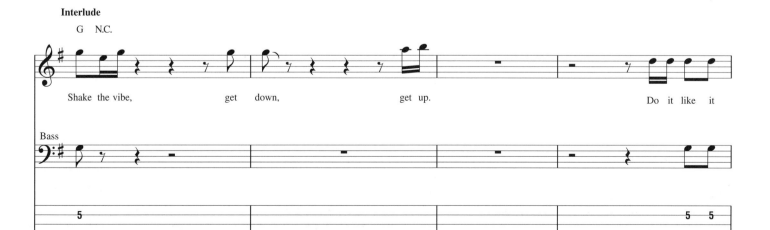

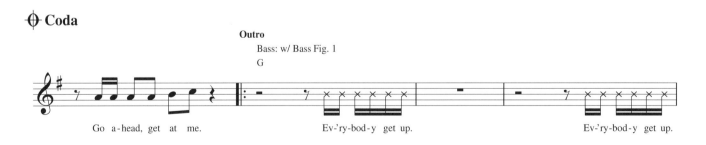

from Maroon 5 - *Overexposed*
Daylight
Words and Music by Adam Levine, Max Martin, Sam Martin and Mason Levy

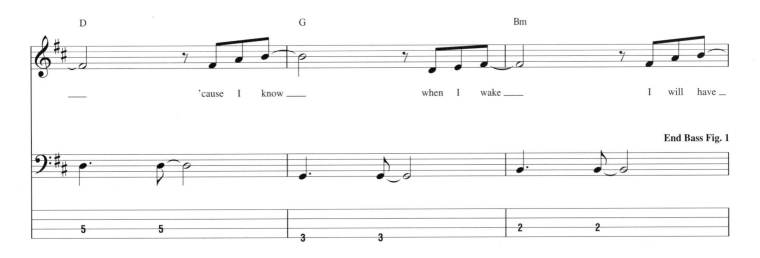

Copyright © 2012 by Universal Music - Careers, Sudgee Music, MXM Music AB,
Artist Publishing Group West, Sam Martin Music Publishing and Mason Levy Productions
All Rights for Sudgee Music Administered by Universal Music - Careers
All Rights for MXM Music AB Administered by Kobalt Songs Music Publishing
All Rights for Artist Publishing Group West, Sam Martin Music Publishing and Mason Levy Productions Administered by WB Music Corp.
International Copyright Secured   All Rights Reserved

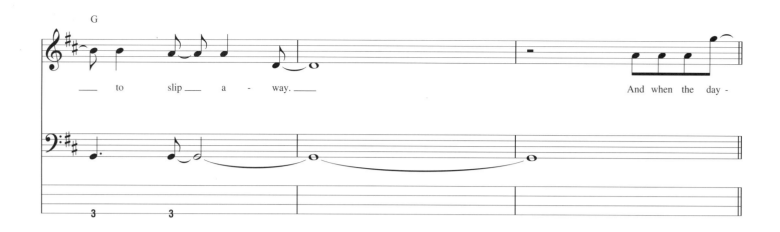

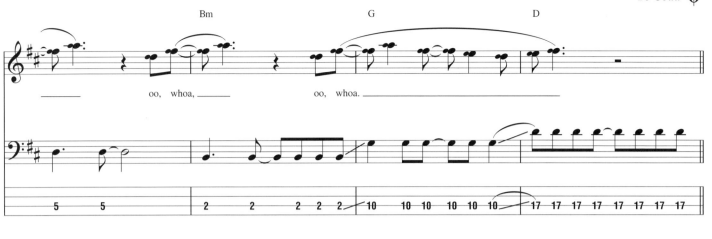

Verse
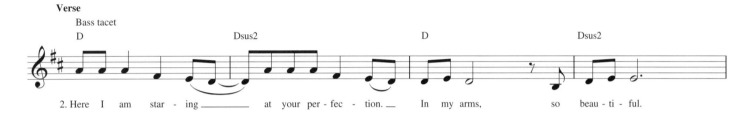
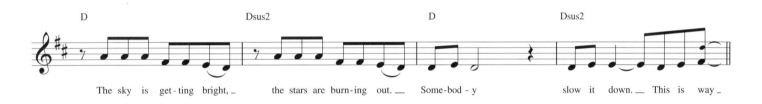

Pre-Chorus

D.S. al Coda
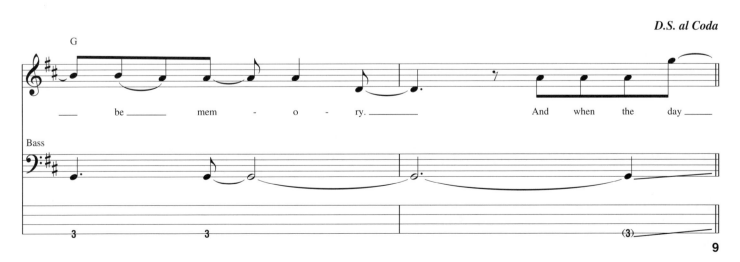

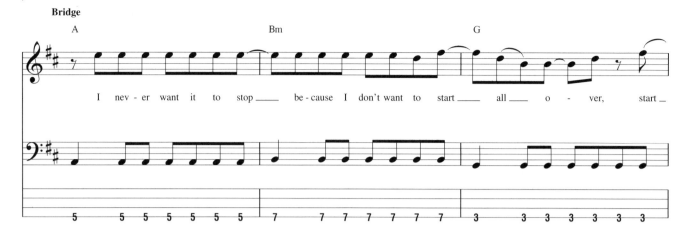

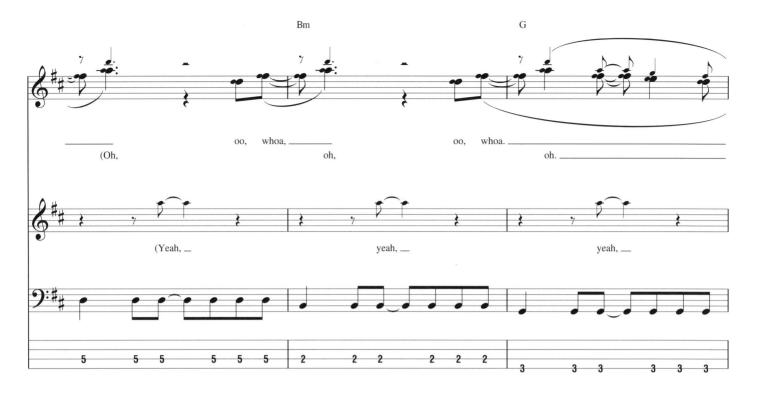

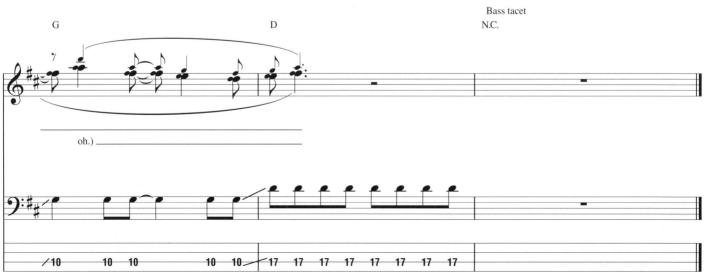

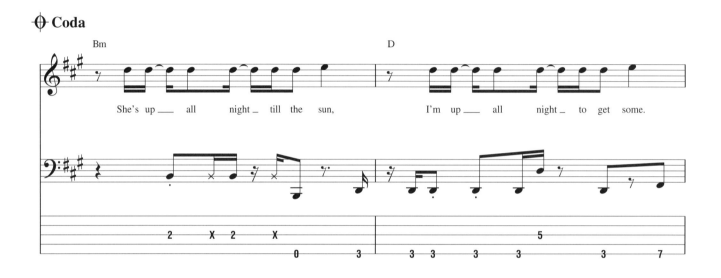

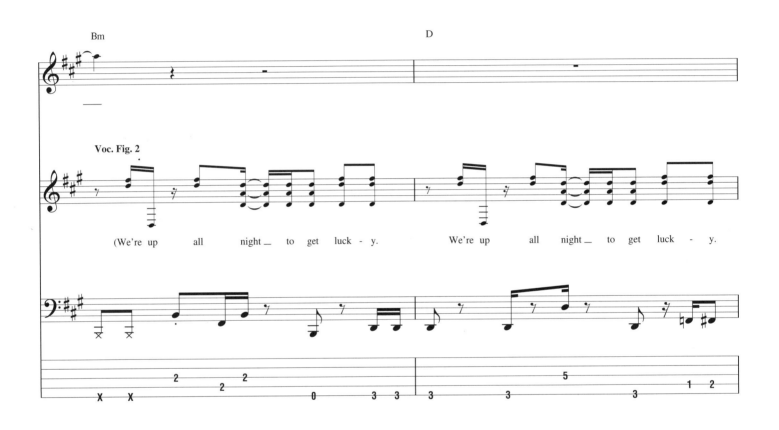

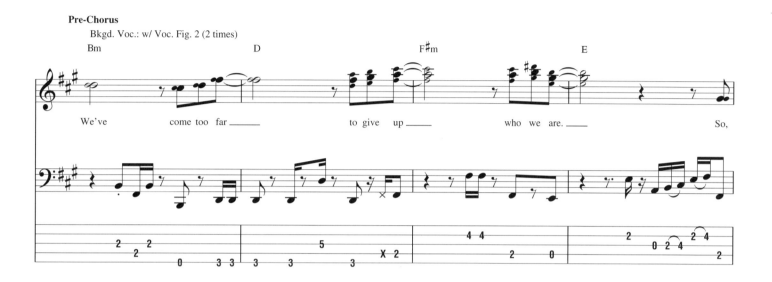

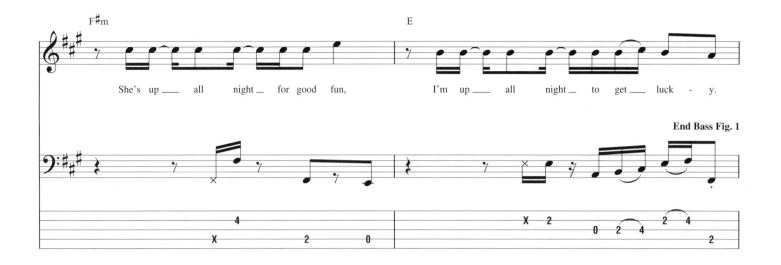
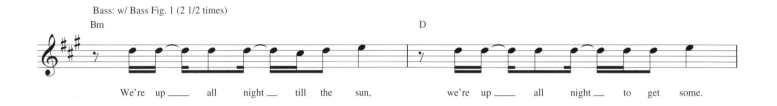

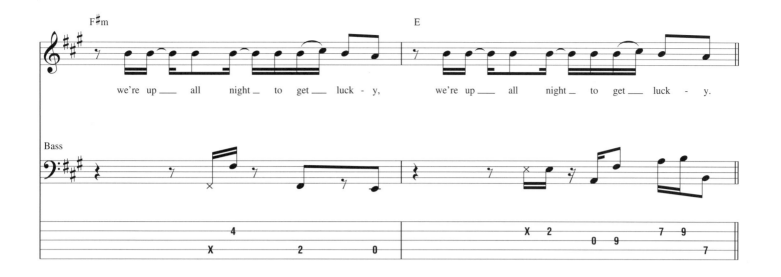
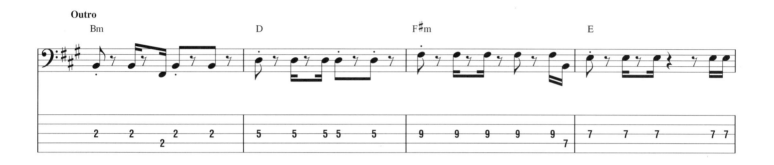

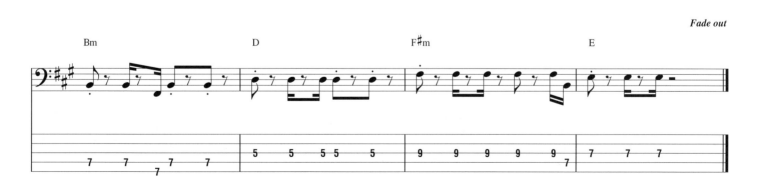

from Volbeat - *Outlaw Gentlemen & Shady Ladies*

The Hangman's Body Count

Words and Music by Michael Poulsen

Tune down 1 step:
(low to high) D-G-C-F

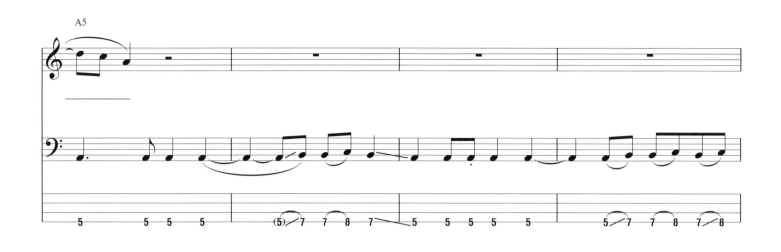

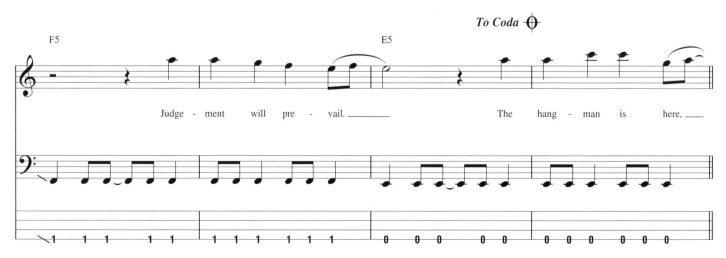

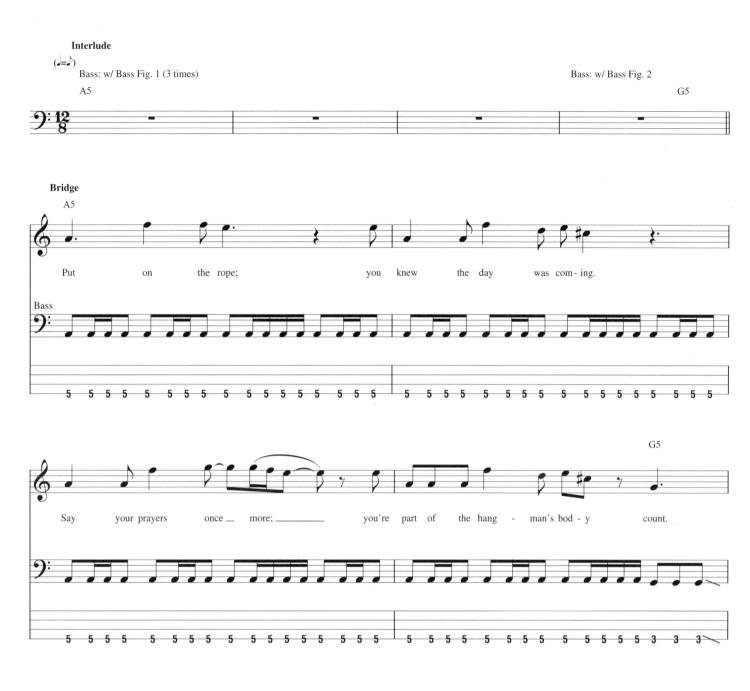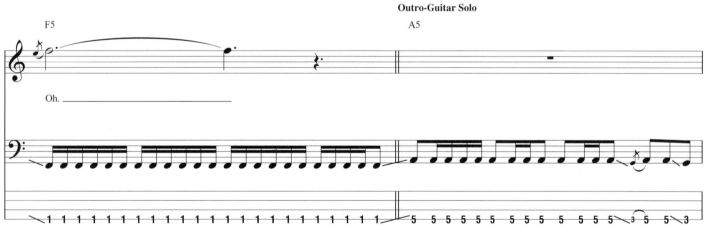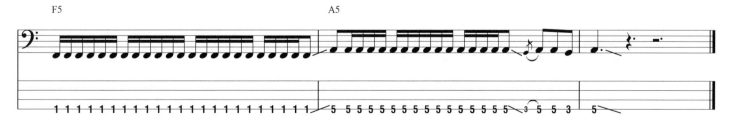

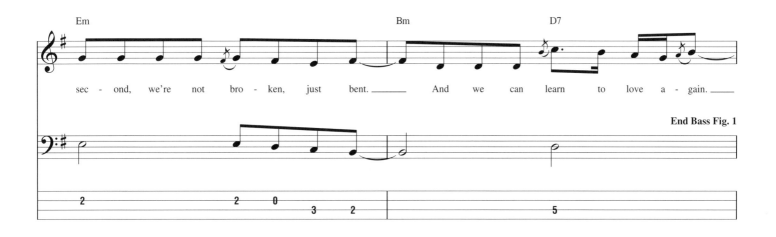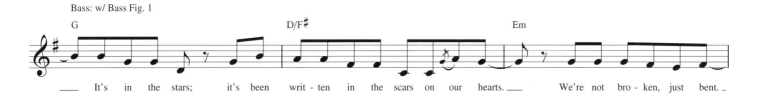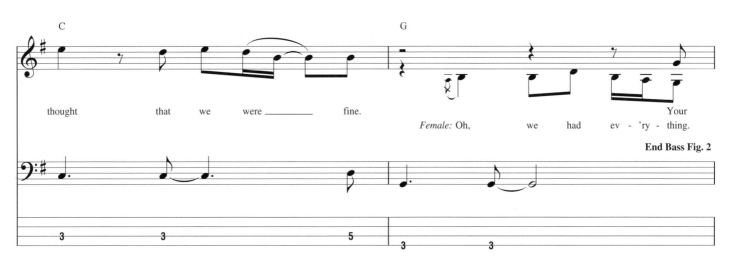

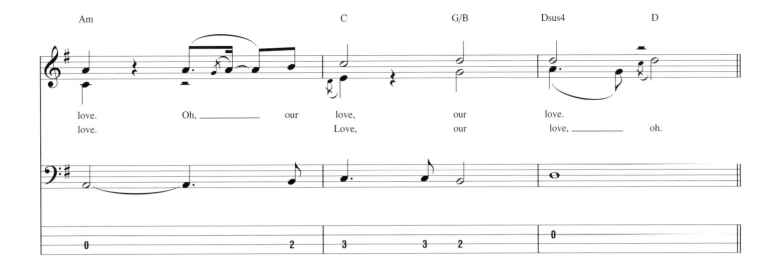

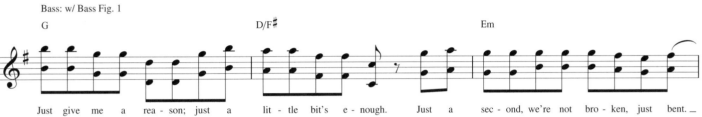

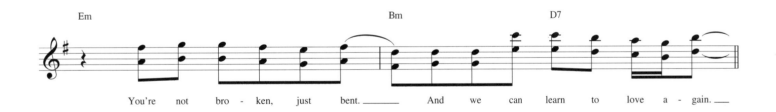

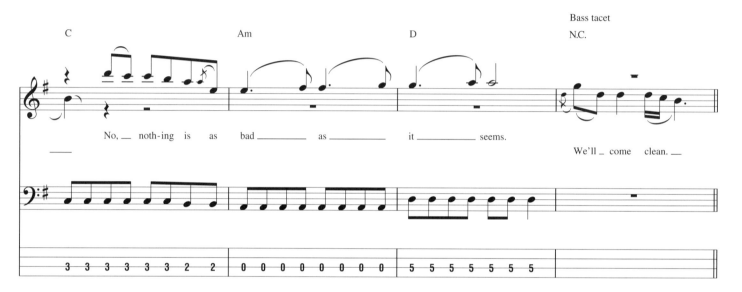
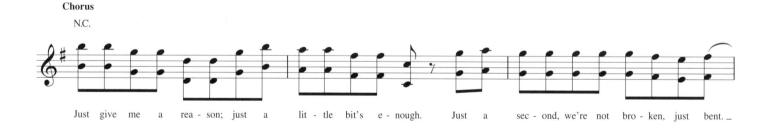

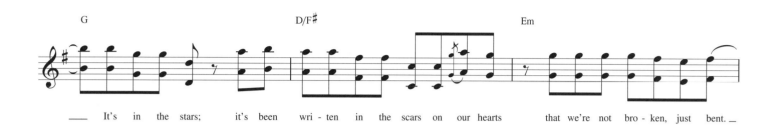
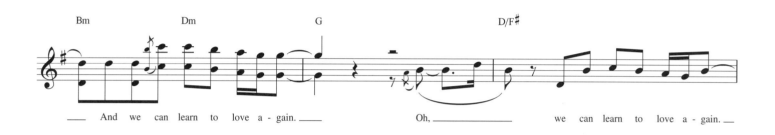
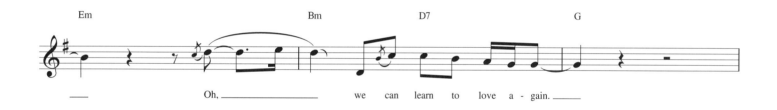

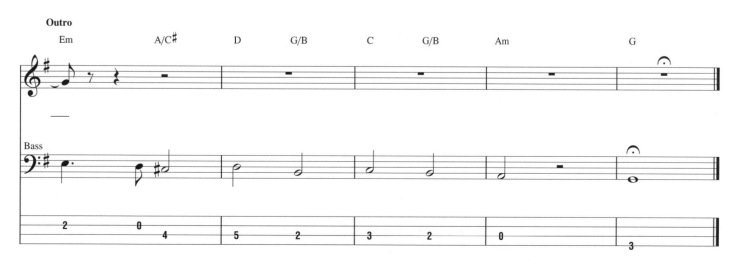

from Bruno Mars - *Unorthodox Jukebox*

Locked Out of Heaven

Words and Music by Bruno Mars, Ari Levine and Philip Lawrence

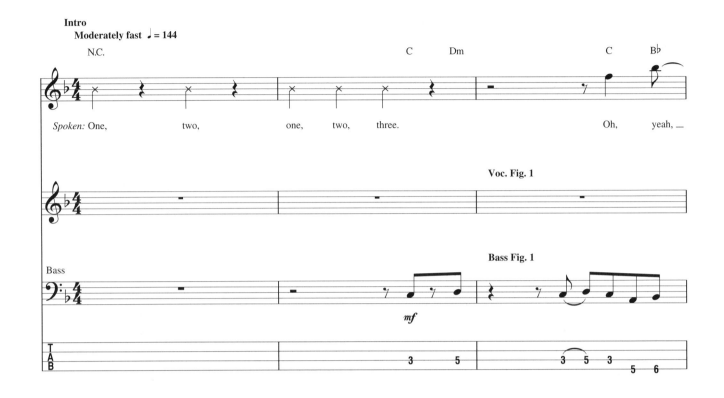

© 2012 BMG GOLD SONGS, MARS FORCE MUSIC, UNIVERSAL MUSIC CORP., TOY PLANE MUSIC,
NORTHSIDE INDEPENDENT MUSIC PUBLISHING LLC, THOU ART THE HUNGER, WB MUSIC CORP. and ROC NATION MUSIC
All Rights for BMG GOLD SONGS and MARS FORCE MUSIC Administered by BMG RIGHTS MANAGEMENT (US) LLC
All Rights for TOY PLANE MUSIC Controlled and Administered by UNIVERSAL MUSIC CORP.
All Rights for THOU ART THE HUNGER Administered by NORTHSIDE INDEPENDENT MUSIC PUBLISHING LLC
All Rights for ROC NATION MUSIC Administered by WB MUSIC CORP.
All Rights Reserved   Used by Permission

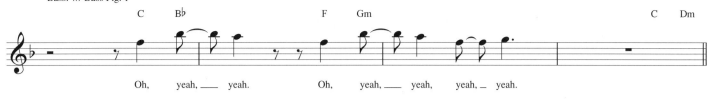
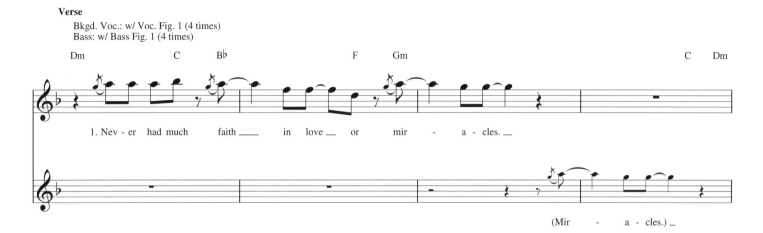
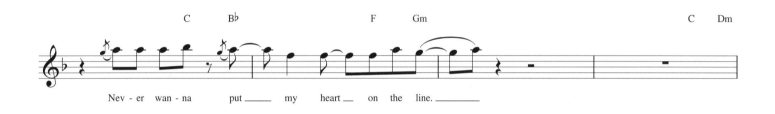
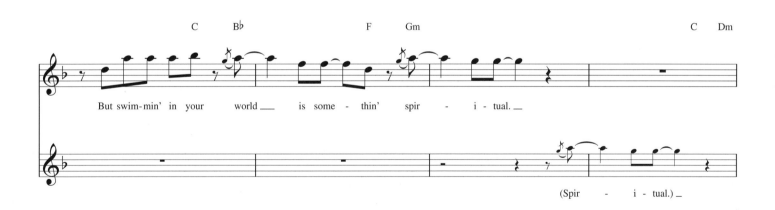
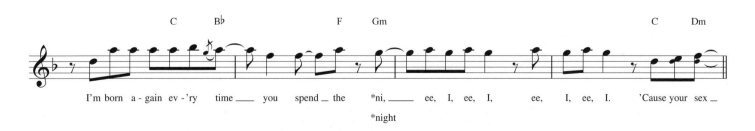

35

Pre-Chorus

*shows

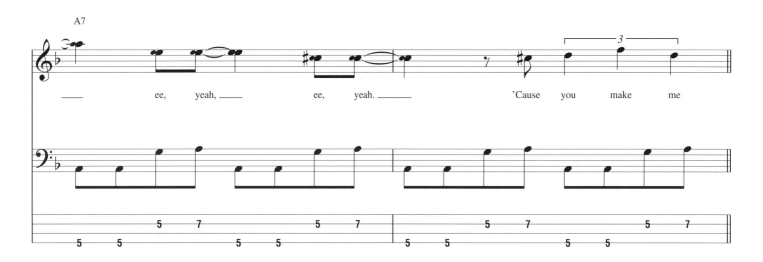

Chorus

**w/ echo set for half-note regeneration w/ 1 repeat where indicated, next 16 meas.

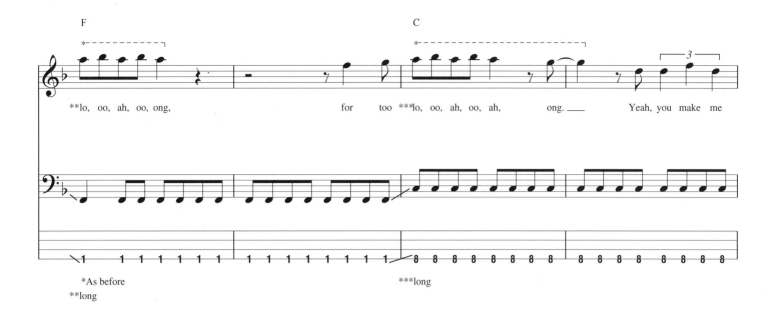
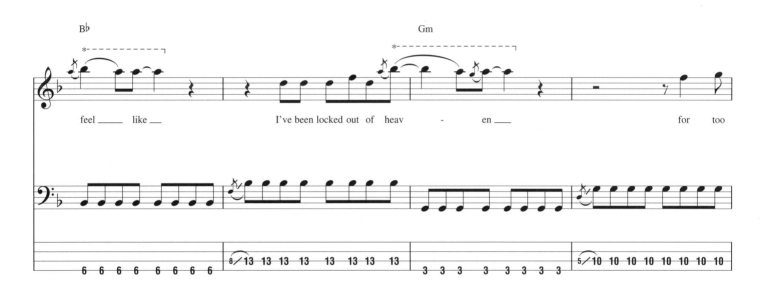
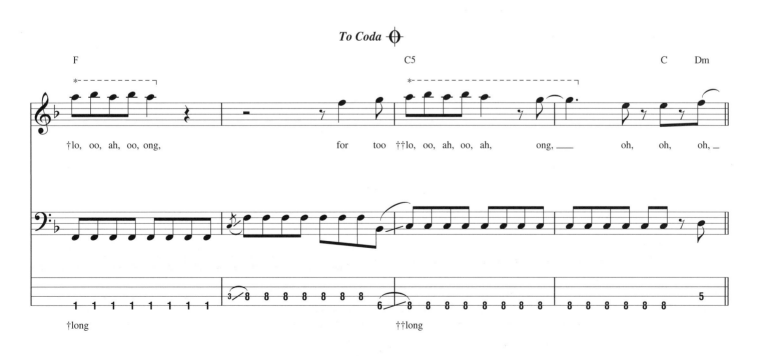

Interlude

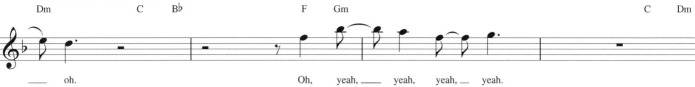

Verse

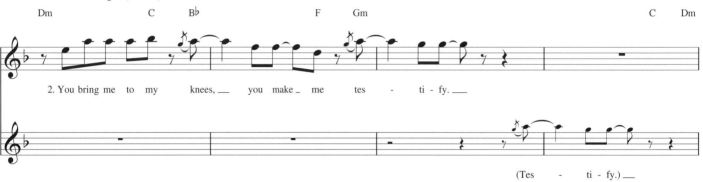

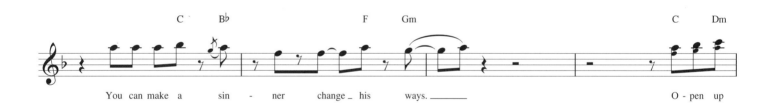

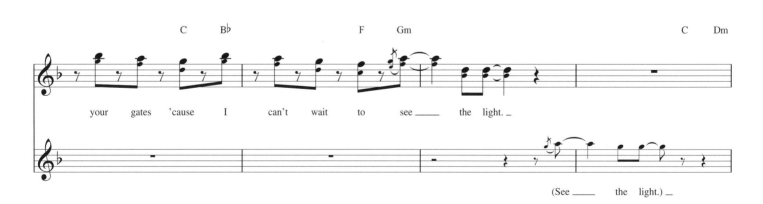

D.S. al Coda

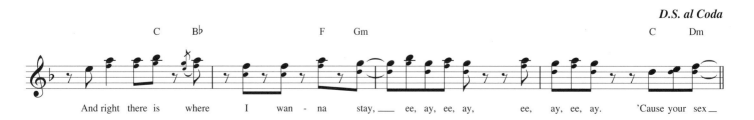

Coda

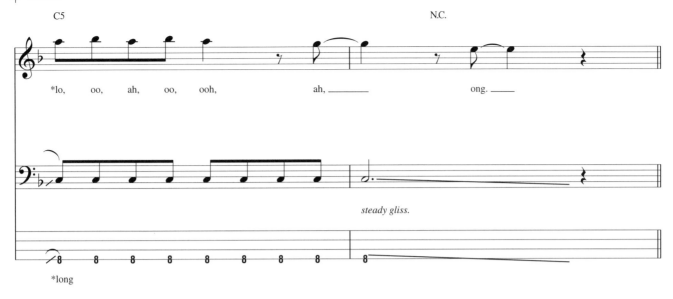

*long

Bridge

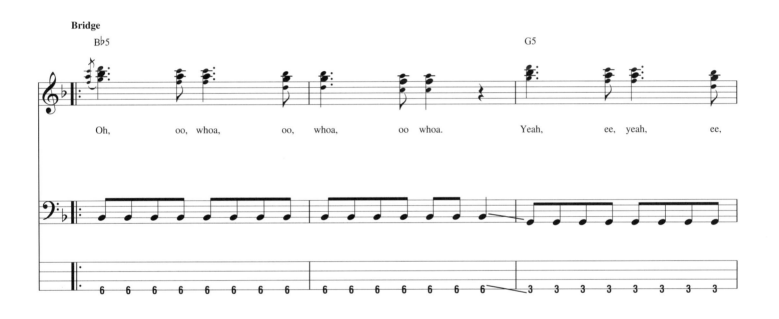

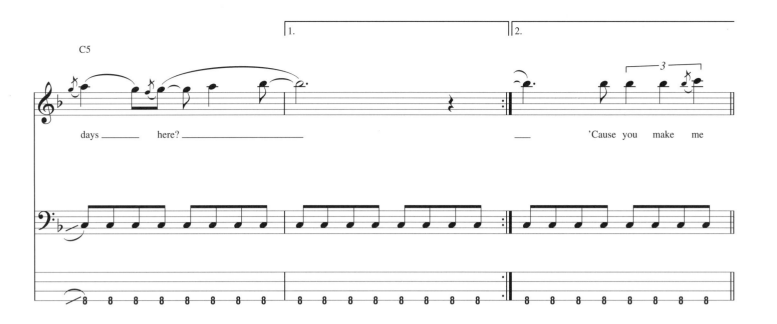

Chorus

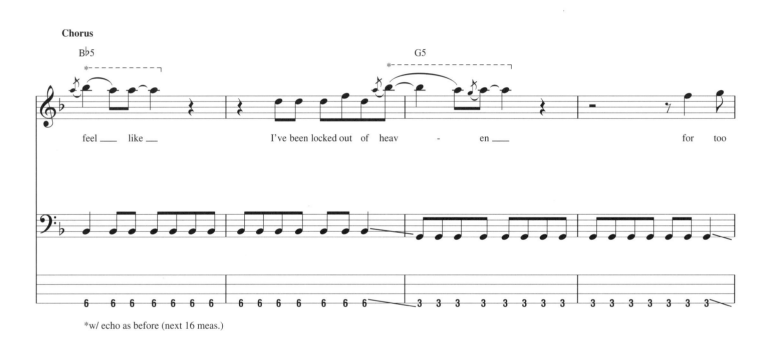

*w/ echo as before (next 16 meas.)

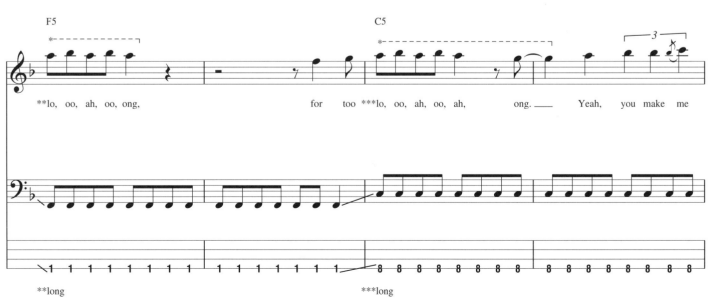

**long   ***long

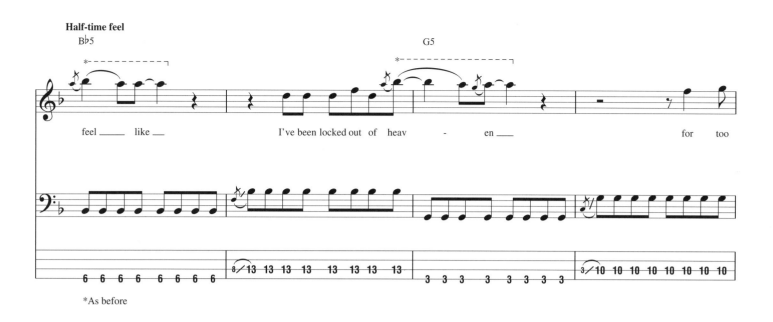

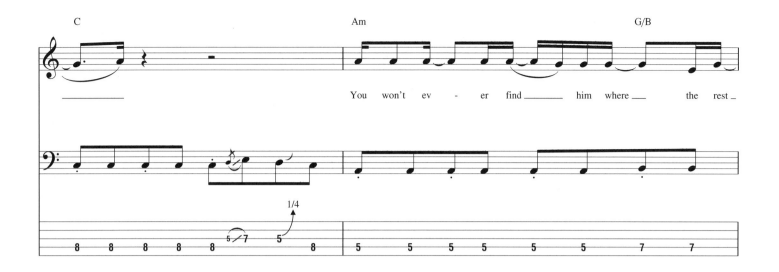

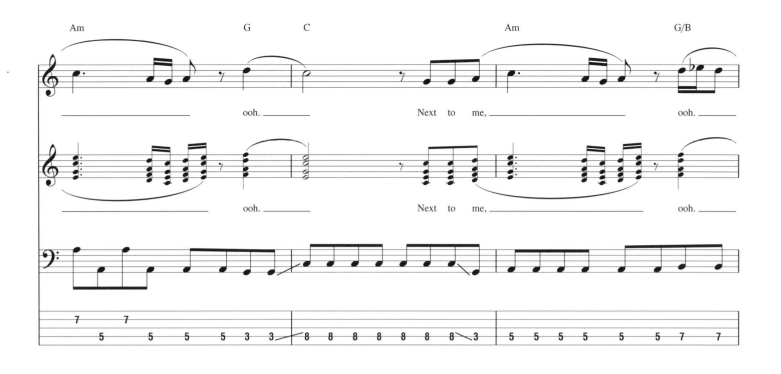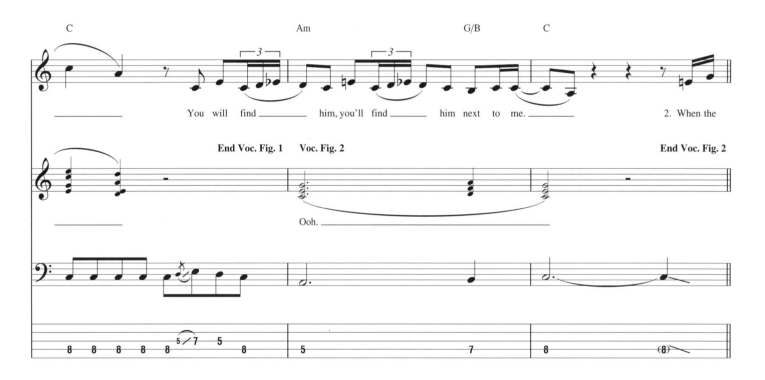

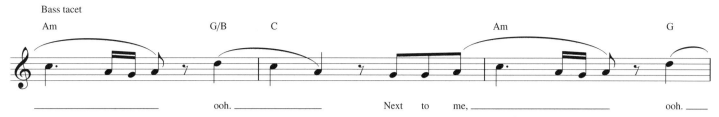

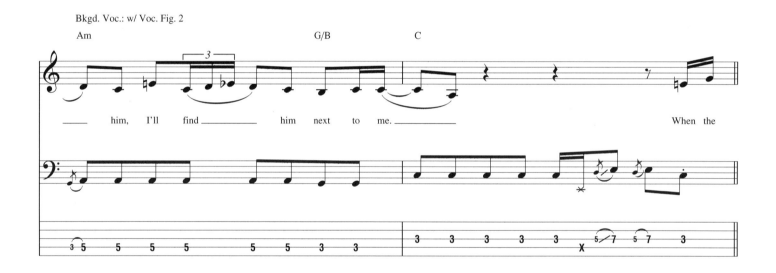

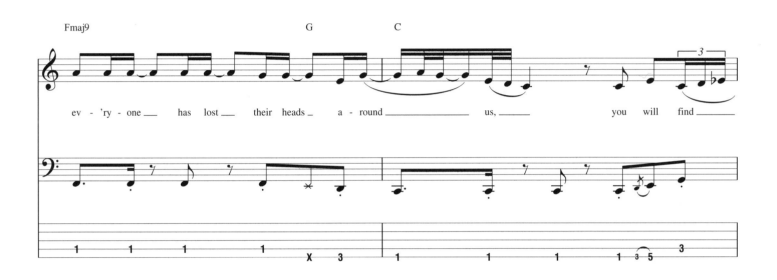

from Muse - *The 2nd Law*
Panic Station
Words and Music by Matthew Bellamy

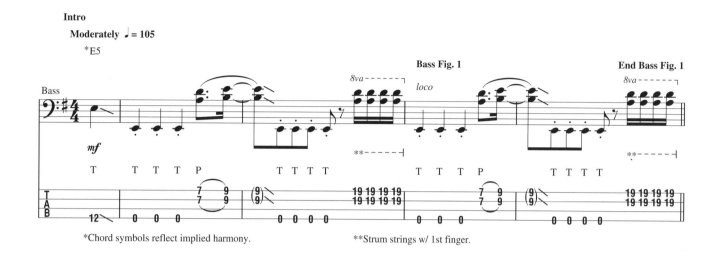

*Chord symbols reflect implied harmony.   **Strum strings w/ 1st finger.

1. You won't get much clos-er___ un-til you sac-ri-fice it all, all.
2. Doubts will try to break you___ un-leash your heart and soul, soul.

***w/ slapback echo

You won't get to taste it___ with your face a-gainst the wall, wall, wall.
Trou-ble will sur-round you,___ start tak-ing some con-trol, trol!___

†As before

Get up and com-mit, show___ the pow-er trapped with-in, in,___ in.
Stand up and de-liv-er___ your wild-est fan-ta-sy, see,___ see. Do

††As before
†††As before

© 2012 HEWRATE LIMITED
All Rights in the U.S. and Canada Administered by WB MUSIC CORP.
All Rights Reserved   Used by Permission

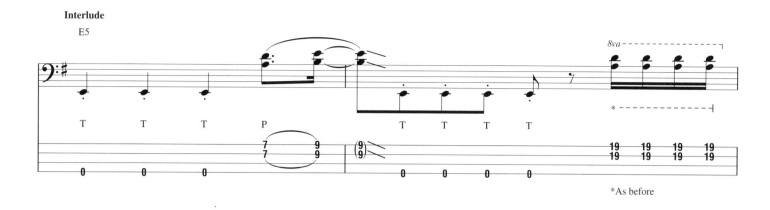

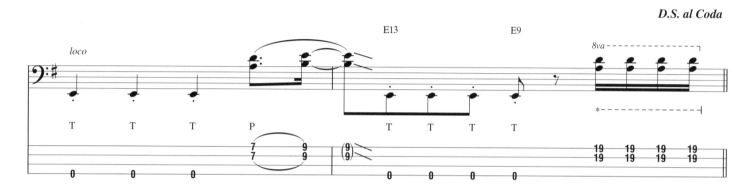

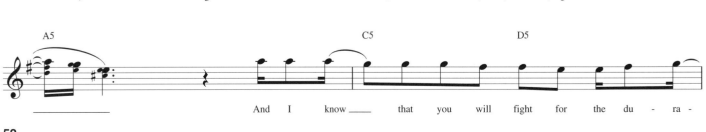

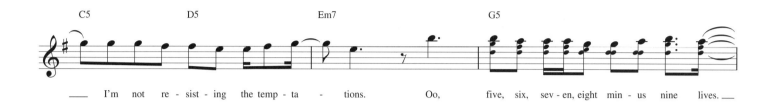
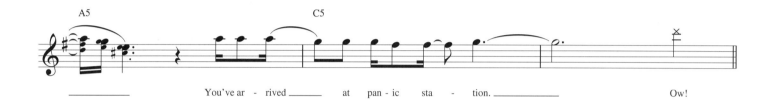

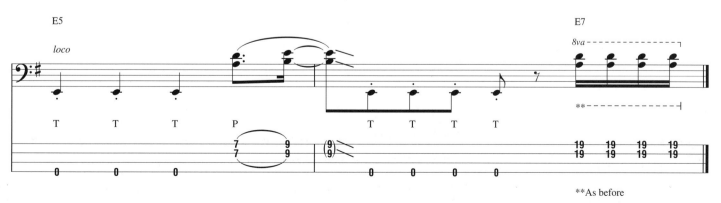

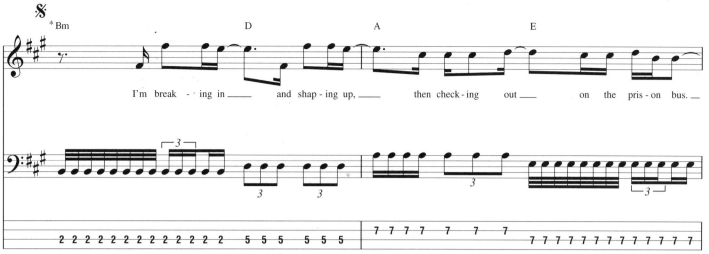

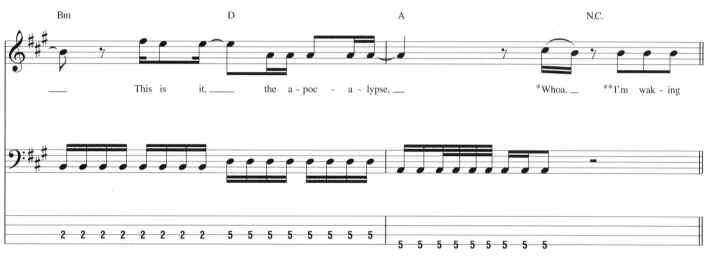

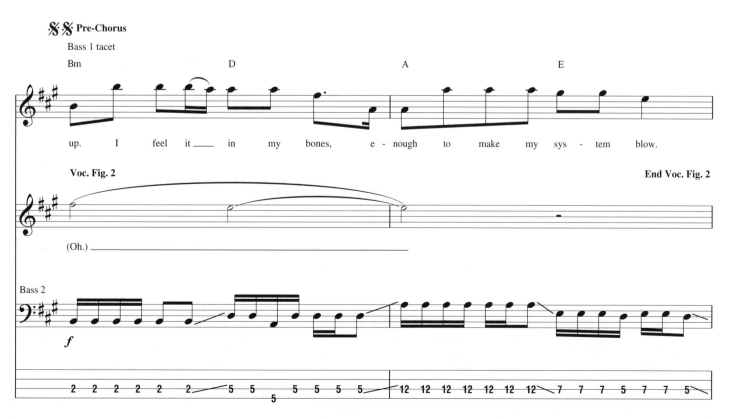

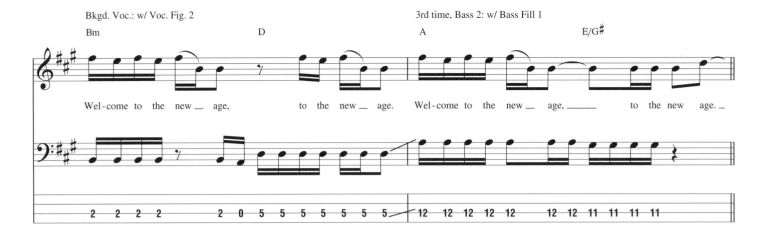
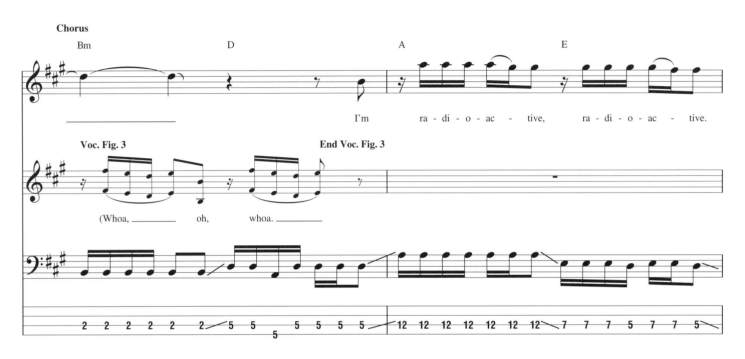
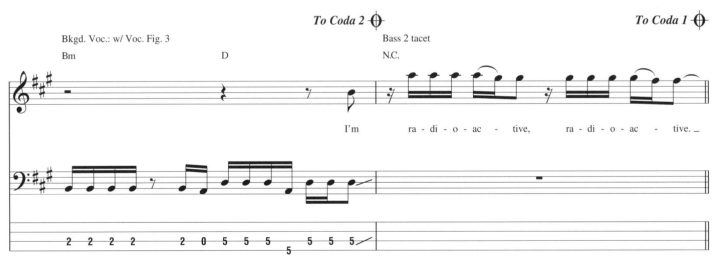
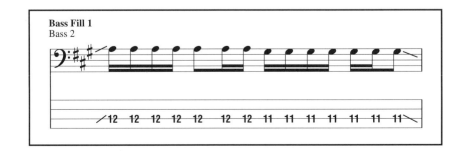

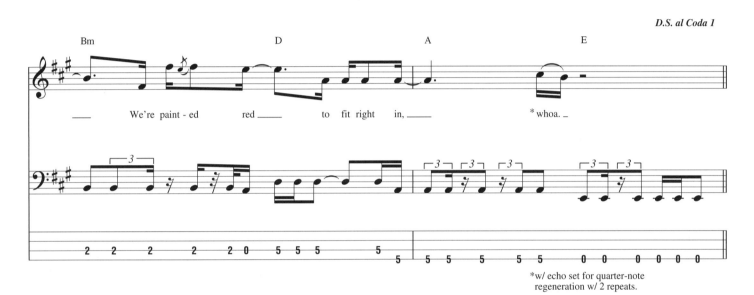

*w/ echo set for quarter-note regeneration w/ 2 repeats.

⊕ Coda 1

Bridge

⊕ Coda 2

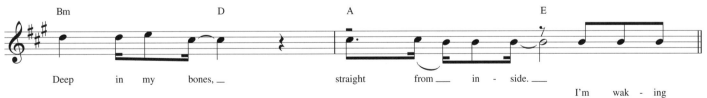

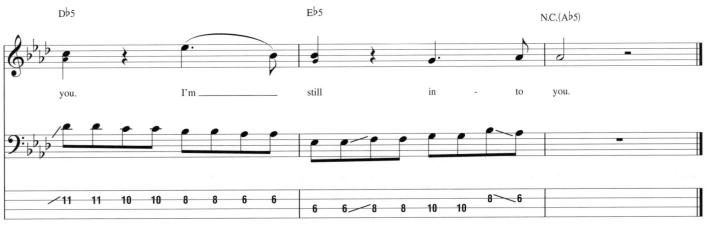

from Justin Timberlake - *The 20/20 Experience*

Suit & Tie

Words and Music by Justin Timberlake, James Fauntleroy, Shawn Carter, Jerome Harmon, Terrance Stubbs, Johnny Wilson, Charles Still and Tim Mosley

5-string bass, Drop A tuning:
(low to high) A-E-A-D-G

Copyright © 2013 by Universal Music - Z Tunes LLC, Tennman Tunes, Almo Music Corp., Underdog West Songs, Fauntleroy Music, WB Music Corp.,
Carter Boys Music, Warner-Tamerlane Publishing Corp., Jerome Harmon Productions, Dynatone Publishing Company and VB Rising Publishing
All Rights for Tennman Tunes Administered by Universal Music - Z Tunes LLC
All Rights for Underdog West Songs and Fauntleroy Music Controlled and Administered by Almo Music Corp.
All Rights for Carter Boys Music Administered by WB Music Corp.
All Rights for Jerome Harmon Productions Administered by Warner-Tamerlane Publishing Corp.
All Rights for Dynatone Publishing Company Administered by Unichappell Music Inc.
All Rights for VB Rising Publishing Administered by ole
International Copyright Secured   All Rights Reserved
-contains a sample of "Sho Nuff" by Terrance Stubbs, Johnny Wilson and Charles Still,
© 1974 (Renewed) Dynatone Publishing Company

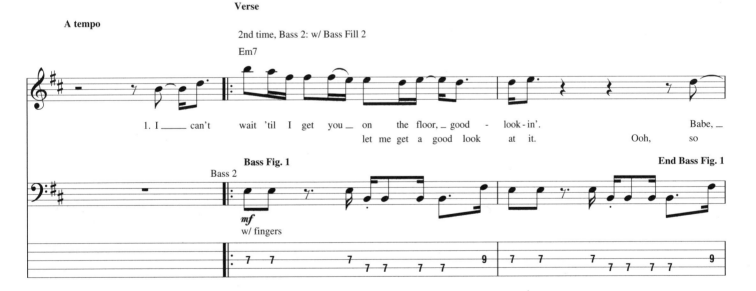

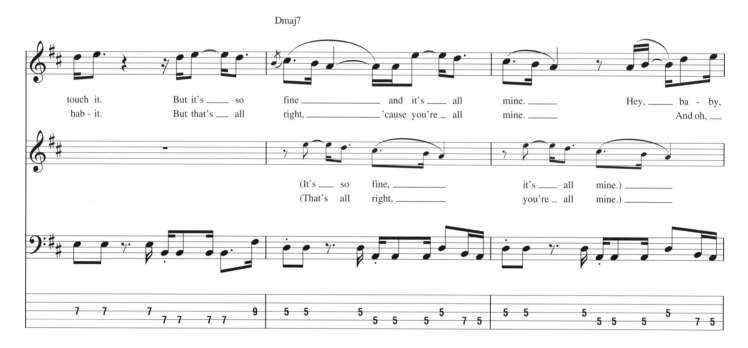
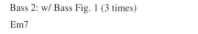

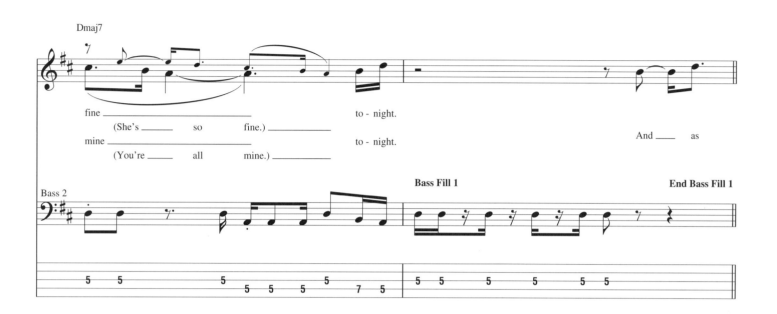

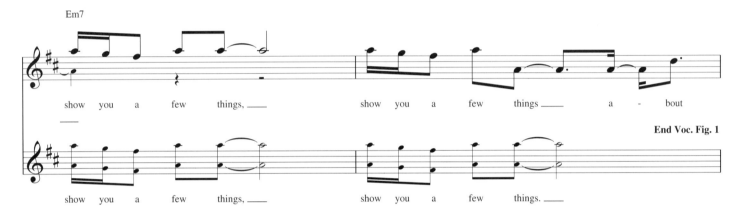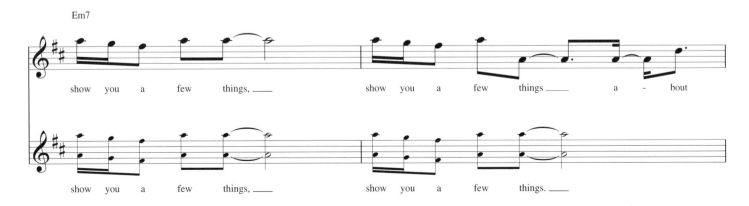

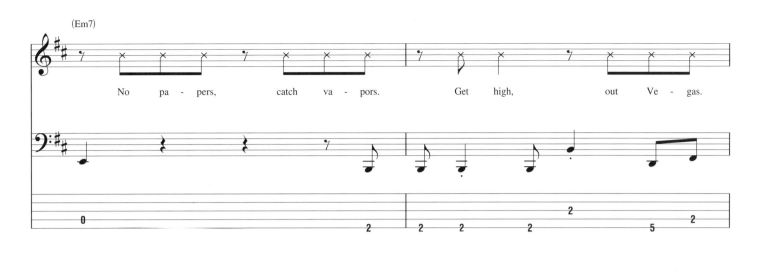
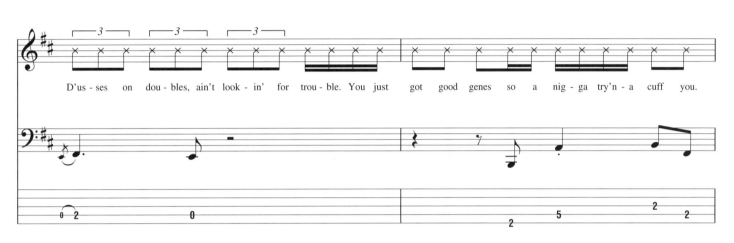
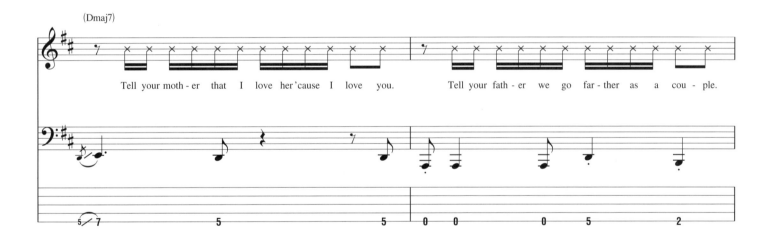
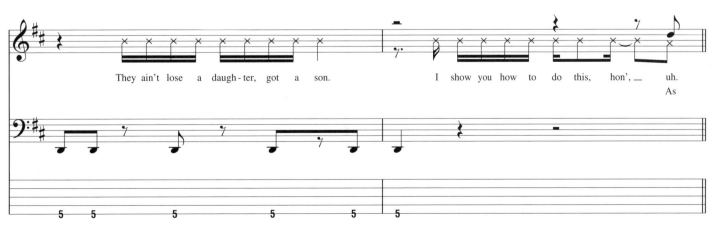

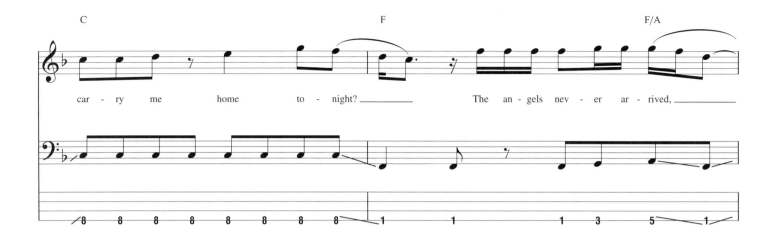

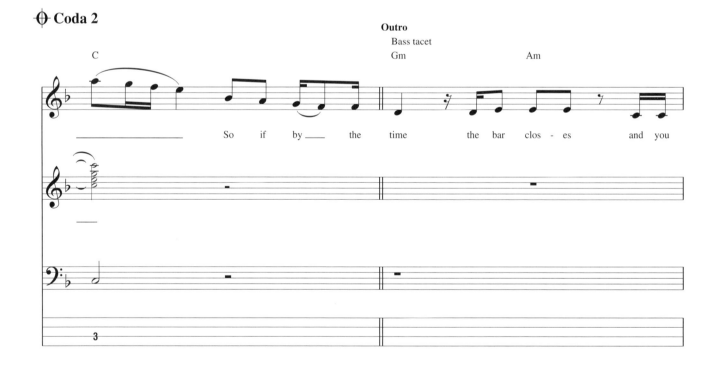

BASS NOTATION LEGEND

Bass music can be notated two different ways: on a *musical staff*, and in *tablature*.

THE MUSICAL STAFF shows pitches and rhythms and is divided by bar lines into measures. Pitches are named after the first seven letters of the alphabet.

TABLATURE graphically represents the bass fingerboard. Each horizontal line represents a string, and each number represents a fret.

3rd string, open   2nd string, 2nd fret   1st & 2nd strings open, played together

HAMMER-ON: Strike the first (lower) note with one finger, then sound the higher note (on the same string) with another finger by fretting it without picking.

PULL-OFF: Place both fingers on the notes to be sounded. Strike the first note and without picking, pull the finger off to sound the second (lower) note.

LEGATO SLIDE: Strike the first note and then slide the same fret-hand finger up or down to the second note. The second note is not struck.

SHIFT SLIDE: Same as legato slide, except the second note is struck.

TRILL: Very rapidly alternate between the notes indicated by continuously hammering on and pulling off.

TREMOLO PICKING: The note is picked as rapidly and continuously as possible.

VIBRATO: The string is vibrated by rapidly bending and releasing the note with the fretting hand.

SHAKE: Using one finger, rapidly alternate between two notes on one string by sliding either a half-step above or below.

NATURAL HARMONIC: Strike the note while the fret hand lightly touches the string directly over the fret indicated.

MUFFLED STRINGS: A percussive sound is produced by laying the fret hand across the string(s) without depressing them and striking them with the pick hand.

BEND: Strike the note and bend up the interval shown.

BEND AND RELEASE: Strike the note and bend up as indicated, then release back to the original note. Only the first note is struck.

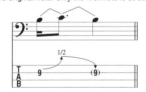

RIGHT-HAND TAP: Hammer ("tap") the fret indicated with the "pick-hand" index or middle finger and pull off to the note fretted by the fret hand.

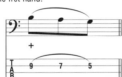

LEFT-HAND TAP: Hammer ("tap") the fret indicated with the "fret-hand" index or middle finger.

SLAP: Strike ("slap") string with right-hand thumb.

POP: Snap ("pop") string with right-hand index or middle finger.

Additional Musical Definitions

 (accent)   • Accentuate note (play it louder).

 (accent)   • Accentuate note with great intensity.

 (staccato)   • Play the note short.

     • Downstroke

V   • Upstroke

D.S. al Coda   • Go back to the sign (𝄋), then play until the measure marked "*To Coda*," then skip to the section labelled "*Coda*."

D.C. al Fine   • Go back to the beginning of the song and play until the measure marked "*Fine*" (end).

Bass Fig.   • Label used to recall a recurring pattern.

Fill   • Label used to identify a brief melodic figure which is to be inserted into the arrangement.

tacet   • Instrument is silent (drops out).

   • Repeat measures between signs.

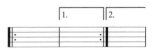   • When a repeated section has different endings, play the first ending only the first time and the second ending only the second time.

NOTE: Tablature numbers in parentheses mean:
1. The note is being sustained over a system (note in standard notation is tied), or
2. The note is sustained, but a new articulation (such as a hammer-on, pull-off, slide or vibrato) begins.

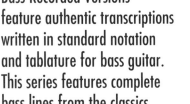

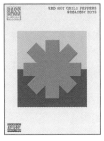

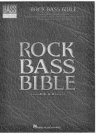

Bass Recorded Versions feature authentic transcriptions written in standard notation and tablature for bass guitar. This series features complete bass lines from the classics to contemporary superstars.

25 All-Time Rock Bass Classics
00690445 / $14.95

25 Essential Rock Bass Classics
00690210 / $15.95

Aerosmith Bass Collection
00690413 / $17.95

Avenged Sevenfold – Nightmare
00691054 / $19.99

Best of Victor Bailey
00690718 / $19.95

Bass Tab 1990-1999
00690400 / $16.95

Bass Tab 1999-2000
00690404 / $14.95

Bass Tab White Pages
00690508 / $29.99

The Beatles Bass Lines
00690170 / $14.95

The Beatles 1962-1966
00690556 / $18.99

The Beatles 1967-1970
00690557 / $19.99

Best Bass Rock Hits
00694803 / $12.95

Black Sabbath – We Sold Our Soul for Rock 'N' Roll
00660116 / $17.95

The Best of Blink 182
00690549 / $18.95

Blues Bass Classics
00690291 / $14.95

Boston Bass Collection
00690935 / $19.95

The Best of Eric Clapton
00660187 / $19.95

Stanley Clarke Collection
00672307 / $19.95

Funk Bass Bible
00690744 / $19.95

Hard Rock Bass Bible
00690746 / $17.95

Jimi Hendrix – Are You Experienced?
00690371 / $17.95

Incubus – Morning View
00690639 / $17.95

Iron Maiden Bass Anthology
00690867 / $22.99

Jazz Bass Classics
00102070 / $16.99

Best of Kiss for Bass
00690080 / $19.95

Lynyrd Skynyrd – All-Time Greatest Hits
00690956 / $19.99

Bob Marley Bass Collection
00690568 / $19.95

Mastodon – Crack the Skye
00691007 / $19.99

Best of Marcus Miller
00690811 / $22.99

Motown Bass Classics
00690253 / $14.95

Mudvayne – Lost & Found
00690798 / $19.95

Nirvana Bass Collection
00690066 / $19.95

No Doubt – Tragic Kingdom
00120112 / $22.95

The Offspring – Greatest Hits
00690809 / $17.95

Jaco Pastorius – Greatest Jazz Fusion Bass Player
00690421 / $19.99

The Essential Jaco Pastorius
00690420 / $19.99

Pearl Jam – Ten
00694882 / $16.99

Pink Floyd – Dark Side of the Moon
00660172 / $14.95

The Best of Police
00660207 / $14.95

Pop/Rock Bass Bible
00690747 / $17.95

Queen – The Bass Collection
00690065 / $19.99

R&B Bass Bible
00690745 / $17.95

Rage Against the Machine
00690248 / $17.99

The Best of Red Hot Chili Peppers
00695285 / $24.95

Red Hot Chili Peppers – Blood Sugar Sex Magik
00690064 / $19.95

Red Hot Chili Peppers – By the Way
00690585 / $19.95

Red Hot Chili Peppers – Californication
00690390 / $19.95

Red Hot Chili Peppers – Greatest Hits
00690675 / $18.95

Red Hot Chili Peppers – I'm with You
00691167 / $22.99

Red Hot Chili Peppers – One Hot Minute
00690091 / $18.95

Red Hot Chili Peppers – Stadium Arcadium
00690853 / $24.95

Red Hot Chili Peppers – Stadium Arcadium: Deluxe Edition
Book/2-CD Pack
00690863 / $39.95

Rock Bass Bible
00690446 / $19.95

Rolling Stones
00690256 / $16.95

Stevie Ray Vaughan – Lightnin' Blues 1983-1987
00694778 / $19.95

Best of ZZ Top for Bass
00691069 / $22.99

HAL•LEONARD® CORPORATION
7777 W. BLUEMOUND RD. P.O. BOX 13819
MILWAUKEE, WISCONSIN 53213

Visit Hal Leonard Online at
www.halleonard.com

Prices, contents & availability subject to change without notice.
Some products may not be available outside the U.S.A.

0313

The Bass Play-Along™ Series will help you play your favorite songs quickly and easily! Just follow the tab, listen to the CD to hear how the bass should sound, and then play along using the separate backing tracks. The melody and lyrics are also included in the book in case you want to sing, or to simply help you follow along. The CD is enhanced so you can use your computer to adjust the recording to any tempo without changing pitch!

 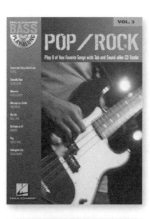 

 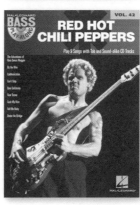 

1. Rock
00699674 Book/CD Pack............$12.95

2. R&B
00699675 Book/CD Pack............$14.99

3. Pop/Rock
00699677 Book/CD Pack............$12.95

4. '90s Rock
00699679 Book/CD Pack............$12.95

5. Funk
00699680 Book/CD Pack............$12.95

6. Classic Rock
00699678 Book/CD Pack............$12.95

7. Hard Rock
00699676 Book/CD Pack............$14.95

8. Punk Rock
00699813 Book/CD Pack............$12.95

9. Blues
00699817 Book/CD Pack............$14.99

10. Jimi Hendrix Smash Hits
00699815 Book/CD Pack............$16.95

11. Country
00699818 Book/CD Pack............$12.95

12. Punk Classics
00699814 Book/CD Pack............$12.99

13. Lennon & McCartney
00699816 Book/CD Pack............$14.99

14. Modern Rock
00699821 Book/CD Pack............$14.99

15. Mainstream Rock
00699822 Book/CD Pack............$14.99

16. '80s Metal
00699825 Book/CD Pack............$16.99

17. Pop Metal
00699826 Book/CD Pack............$14.99

18. Blues Rock
00699828 Book/CD Pack............$14.99

19. Steely Dan
00700203 Book/CD Pack............$16.99

20. The Police
00700270 Book/CD Pack............$14.99

21. Rock Band – Modern Rock
00700705 Book/CD Pack............$14.95

22. Rock Band – Classic Rock
00700706 Book/CD Pack............$14.95

23. Pink Floyd – Dark Side of The Moon
00700847 Book/CD Pack............$14.99

24. Weezer
00700960 Book/CD Pack............$14.99

25. Nirvana
00701047 Book/CD Pack............$14.99

26. Black Sabbath
00701180 Book/CD Pack............$16.99

27. Kiss
00701181 Book/CD Pack............$14.99

28. The Who
00701182 Book/CD Pack............$14.99

29. Eric Clapton
00701183 Book/CD Pack............$14.99

30. Early Rock
00701184 Book/CD Pack............$15.99

31. The 1970s
00701185 Book/CD Pack............$14.99

32. Disco
00701186 Book/CD Pack............$14.99

33. Christmas Hits
00701197 Book/CD Pack............$12.99

34. Easy Songs
00701480 Book/CD Pack............$12.99

35. Bob Marley
00701702 Book/CD Pack............$14.99

36. Aerosmith
00701886 Book/CD Pack............$14.99

37. Modern Worship
00701920 Book/CD Pack............$12.99

38. Avenged Sevenfold
00702386 Book/CD Pack............$16.99

40. AC/DC
14041594 Book/CD Pack............$16.99

41. U2
00702582 Book/CD Pack............$16.99

42. Red Hot Chili Peppers
00702991 Book/CD Pack............$19.99

43. Paul McCartney
00703079 Book/CD Pack............$16.99

44. Megadeth
00703080 Book/CD Pack............$16.99

45. Slipknot
00703201 Book/CD Pack............$16.99

FOR MORE INFORMATION, SEE YOUR LOCAL MUSIC DEALER,
OR WRITE TO:

7777 W. BLUEMOUND RD. P.O. BOX 13819 MILWAUKEE, WI 53213

Visit Hal Leonard Online at **www.halleonard.com**
Prices, contents, and availability subject to change without notice.

0313

BASS BUILDERS

A series of technique book/CD packages created for the purposeful building and development of your chops. Each volume is written by an expert in that particular technique. And with the inclusion of audio, the added dimension of hearing exactly how to play particular grooves and techniques make these truly like private lessons.

BASS AEROBICS
by Jon Liebman
00696437 Book/CD Pack.......................$19.99

BASS FITNESS – AN EXERCISING HANDBOOK
by Josquin des Prés
00660177..$10.99

BASS FOR BEGINNERS
by Glenn Letsch
00695099 Book/CD Pack.......................$19.95

BASS GROOVES
by Jon Liebman
00696028 Book/CD Pack.......................$19.99

BASS IMPROVISATION
by Ed Friedland
00695164 Book/CD Pack.......................$17.95

BLUES BASS
by Jon Liebman
00695235 Book/CD Pack.......................$19.95

BUILDING ROCK BASS LINES
by Ed Friedland
00695692 Book/CD Pack.......................$17.95

BUILDING WALKING BASS LINES
by Ed Friedland
00695008 Book/CD Pack.......................$19.99

RON CARTER – BUILDING JAZZ BASS LINES
00841240 Book/CD Pack.......................$19.95

DICTIONARY OF BASS GROOVES
by Sean Malone
00695266 Book/CD Pack.......................$14.95

EXPANDING WALKING BASS LINES
by Ed Friedland
00695026 Book/CD Pack.......................$19.95

FINGERBOARD HARMONY FOR BASS
by Gary Willis
00695043 Book/CD Pack.......................$17.95

FUNK BASS
by Jon Liebman
00699348 Book/CD Pack.......................$19.99

FUNK/FUSION BASS
by Jon Liebman
00696553 Book/CD Pack.......................$19.95

HIP-HOP BASS
by Josquin des Prés
00695589 Book/CD Pack.......................$14.95

JAZZ BASS
by Ed Friedland
00695084 Book/CD Pack.......................$17.95

JERRY JEMMOTT – BLUES AND RHYTHM & BLUES BASS TECHNIQUE
00695176 Book/CD Pack.......................$17.95

JUMP 'N' BLUES BASS
by Keith Rosier
00695292 Book/CD Pack.......................$16.95

THE LOST ART OF COUNTRY BASS
by Keith Rosier
00695107 Book/CD Pack.......................$19.95

PENTATONIC SCALES FOR BASS
by Ed Friedland
00696224 Book/CD Pack.......................$19.99

REGGAE BASS
by Ed Friedland
00695163 Book/CD Pack.......................$16.95

ROCK BASS
by Jon Liebman
00695083 Book/CD Pack.......................$17.95

'70S FUNK & DISCO BASS
by Josquin des Prés
00695614 Book/CD Pack.......................$15.99

SIMPLIFIED SIGHT-READING FOR BASS
by Josquin des Prés
00695085 Book/CD Pack.......................$17.95

6-STRING BASSICS
by David Gross
00695221 Book/CD Pack.......................$12.95

WORLD BEAT GROOVES FOR BASS
by Tony Cimorosi
00695335 Book/CD Pack.......................$14.95

HAL•LEONARD® CORPORATION
7777 W. BLUEMOUND RD. P.O. BOX 13819 MILWAUKEE, WI 53213

Visit Hal Leonard Online at **www.halleonard.com**

Prices, contents and availability subject to change without notice; All prices are listed in U.S. funds

0313